Original title:
The Chill of Stars

Copyright © 2024 Swan Charm
All rights reserved.

Author: Daisy Dewi
ISBN HARDBACK: 978-9908-52-104-6
ISBN PAPERBACK: 978-9908-52-105-3
ISBN EBOOK: 978-9908-52-106-0

Distant Whispers in the Winter Sky

In the quiet night, stars appear,
Listening closely, voices we hear.
Echoes of dreams, soft like the breeze,
Whispers of wishes carried with ease.

Snowflakes dance in shimmering light,
Painting the world in purest white.
Each flake a story, unique and bright,
Melding together in the still of night.

Moonlight bathes the earth in glow,
Casting shadows where the cold winds blow.
A blanket of silence, serene and deep,
Nature's embrace, a secret to keep.

Time stands still in this tranquil space,
Wonders of winter, a slow-moving grace.
Frozen landscapes, vast and wide,
Where distant whispers and peace abide.

As dawn approaches, the colors ignite,
A tapestry woven of day and night.
With each new dawn, the whispers remain,
In the winter sky, they call out our name.

Celestial Serendipity in Freeze

Under the blanket of winter's fair,
Stars dance above, a cosmic glare.
Dreams collide in an icy embrace,
Serendipity finds its place.

Frozen lakes mirror the night,
Crystals glimmer, catching the light.
With each breath, the cold cuts clear,
Moments held close, warm and dear.

Winds whisper secrets, old as time,
Nature's chorus, a melodious rhyme.
Glimmers of magic in the air,
Invisible threads tangled with care.

Gazing up, we find our way,
Through celestial paths where shadows play.
A world of wonder, within our grasp,
In winter's embrace, we breathe, we clasp.

As twilight descends, the world slows down,
In our hearts, winter's jewel is found.
Celestial serendipity unfolds,
Tales of silence and beauty told.

Shadows and Crystals Alight

In the hush of night, shadows creep,
Crystals glimmer, secrets they keep.
Moonbeams dance on icy ground,
Whispers of magic echo around.

Trees wear coats of shimmering frost,
In this world, nothing is lost.
Each crystal tells a story so bright,
In the embrace of the tranquil night.

Footprints trace paths of gentle dreams,
Reflections sparkle in silent streams.
The air is crisp, the stars in bloom,
Nature breathes life in the cloak of gloom.

Veils of mist weave through the trees,
A symphony sung by the evening breeze.
Shadows twirl as the stars align,
In this moment, everything shines.

Catch the light in a fleeting glance,
Every shadow holds a hidden chance.
In the quiet heart, the magic grows,
Where shadows and crystals softly glow.

When Stars Freeze

When the stars freeze in the velvet sky,
Dreams take flight, then gently die.
Whispers of hope flutter and fade,
In the stillness, memories invade.

The world below turns to frosty stone,
Echoes of laughter, now overthrown.
A blanket of silence smothers the night,
Under frozen whispers, lost in sight.

Lights flicker like forgotten tales,
Chasing shadows on the icy trails.
Time stands still in this glacial dance,
While the universe holds its trance.

Glimmers of time in the glistening void,
In this silence, hearts are toyed.
A chill that wraps around the soul,
In frozen moments, we become whole.

Stars may freeze, but dreams ignite,
In the depths of the frigid night.
Hold on tight, let your spirit soar,
In the frozen sky, there's always more.

Frosty Glimmers of Infinity

Frosty glimmers spark in the air,
Whispers of dreams float everywhere.
A cosmic dance in the midnight hush,
Echoes of stardust, a fervent rush.

Infinity paints the canvas cold,
With tales of wonders yet untold.
Each glimmer holds a secret's key,
Unlocking realms where we long to be.

Through crystal paths, we wander wide,
Each frosty breath, a breathless ride.
The universe sings in crystalline tones,
As frost embraces the hollowed bones.

Light swirls in patterns, serene and bright,
Guiding lost souls through the night.
With whispers woven in stellar threads,
Infinity calls, as the old life sheds.

Hold the glimmer, let it ignite,
A spark of hope in the quiet night.
Frosty dreams bridge the endless space,
In the heart of forever, we find our place.

Twinkling in an Icy Void

Twinkling stars in an icy void,
Whispers of past and future combined.
Time unravels in frosty rapture,
In this stillness, we find our wild capture.

Crystals shimmer, reflecting light,
Dancing softly in the depth of night.
Each moment a shimmering cascade,
In the cosmic womb, futures are laid.

Frosted winds breathe tales profound,
Secrets echo without a sound.
Boundless dreams in the chilling air,
Calling to souls who dare to care.

Embarking on journeys with hope as a guide,
In the icy void, our dreams collide.
Every twinkle a promise anew,
In the depths of night, we see what's true.

So let the stars twinkle and shine,
In this vast void, forever entwined.
For even in darkness, we find our way,
In the icy void, we bravely stay.

Stardust Crystallized in Air

In the night sky, whispers twirl,
From distant suns, a cosmic swirl.
Glimmers dance on velvet blue,
A tapestry of dreams anew.

Crystals form from hopes untold,
A story spun in threads of gold.
Particles rush in vibrant flight,
Each one born from starlit light.

Caught in winds of wonder vast,
Echoes of the heavens past.
In the silence, magic stays,
Guiding souls through endless ways.

Through the void, we chase the gleam,
Feeling time's eternal dream.
Moments shimmer like the dawn,
As stardust paves the path we walk on.

Dreamscape Under Frost

Beneath the veil of sparkling white,
Whispers float in the still of night.
Frozen petals kiss the ground,
In silence, secrets can be found.

Each crystal flake a lullaby,
Softly floating from the sky.
Dreams awaken, drift and sway,
In this land where frostbirds play.

Shadows dance in the moonlit glow,
While icy streams of breezes flow.
Gentle sighs of winter's breath,
Cradle life beneath the death.

Frozen thoughts, a tranquil sea,
In the heart, there's warmth and glee.
Dreamscape whispers, night's embrace,
In every chill, we find our place.

Illuminated Chills of Infinity

Stars ignite the endless night,
With colors twisting, pure delight.
Galaxies spin in silent grace,
Time dissolves in this vast space.

Each pulse of light, a story shared,
In every swirl, a wish declared.
Cascading echoes, soft and bright,
Illuminate our path in flight.

Frosted skies, where whispers hum,
In the stillness dreams become.
Cold embraces warm the heart,
As shadows and the starlight part.

We drift on winds of pure design,
In infinite realms, souls entwine.
A cosmic dance of light and dark,
As we seek that endless spark.

Ghostly Glints from Far Away

In the twilight's soft embrace,
Faint lights flicker, leave no trace.
Whispers from the distant past,
Echo through the night so vast.

Ghostly glints of faded dreams,
Shine like stars in moonlit beams.
Haunting tales of long-lost days,
Guide the heart through misty ways.

Each shimmer tells a tale unsung,
As time unfolds, and life is spun.
Veils of memory drift and sway,
Drawing shadows into play.

In the silence, spirits dance,
Offering us a fleeting glance.
Through the night, a gentle call,
Ghostly glints, we chase them all.

The Frost's Twilight Dance

In the hush of evening's glow,
The frost begins its gentle show.
Crystals twinkle, softly sway,
As twilight grips the closing day.

A breeze whispers through the trees,
Spreading chill upon the leaves.
Nature's art in silver spun,
A silent dance till day is done.

Moonlight casts its silken thread,
Over fields where dreams are tread.
Footsteps crunch on icy ground,
In this quiet, magic found.

Stars awaken in the night,
Witness to the frost's delight.
Every flake a fleeting chance,
Lending grace to twilight's dance.

As shadows meld with fading light,
We embrace the spell of night.
In the stillness, hearts expand,
To the rhythm of the frost's hand.

Luminaries Beneath the Winter's Breath

Underneath the starry dome,
The world wraps in a quilted tome.
Snowflakes fall like whispered dreams,
In the night, a dance of beams.

Frosted trees stand tall and proud,
Veiled in silver, a sacred shroud.
Nature's breath, both soft and bold,
A story etched in winter's cold.

Candles flicker, warmth within,
Against the chill, our hopes begin.
Each glow a beacon in the night,
Guiding souls with gentle light.

The quiet air, a canvas bare,
Awaits the joy we wish to share.
In this moment, hearts unite,
Beneath the skies, so vast, so bright.

As dawn's first blush gives way to day,
We find our path, we find our way.
Together, through the frosty breath,
We live the magic, defy the death.

Ethereal Glistening of a Silent Night

A veil of white, the world adorned,
In silence deep, the day has mourned.
Stars above, twinkling bright,
Glisten softly in the night.

Footsteps echo on the street,
Where frost and shadows gently meet.
Each breath hangs in frosty air,
A silent wish, a whispered prayer.

Moonlight dances on the ground,
In its glow, peace can be found.
Crystalline dreams in stillness sway,
In the night, they softly play.

Branches bend with winter's weight,
Nature's pause, both small and great.
In this moment, lost in thought,
The magic of the night is caught.

As dawn peeks through the glistening haze,
The world awakens, filled with praise.
For in the night, we've found our sight,
In the ethereal glistening light.

A Symphony of Frost and Light

Upon the stage where frost will reign,
Nature plays her sweet refrain.
Dancing shadows, crisp and clear,
A symphony that draws us near.

Each flake a note, so pure, so bright,
Composed within the still of night.
Harmony in every breath,
A fleeting moment, a dance with death.

The quiet hum of winter's chill,
Invites the heart to stop, be still.
In this magic, we find joy,
A symphony no one can destroy.

With each dawn, the music swells,
Nature's voice in myriad bells.
Resonating through the white,
A tapestry of frost and light.

And as the day begins anew,
We carry forth this song so true.
In every heart, a spark ignites,
A symphony of wondrous sights.

Shimmering Icescape of Dreams

In twilight's glow, the edges gleam,
A world adorned in icy theme.
Whispers cold upon the breeze,
Embracing night with frosted ease.

Crystals dance on silver streams,
Reflecting softly all our dreams.
Each step taken, sharp and clear,
Echoes of the night, so near.

Mountains rise in silent pride,
Wrapped in blankets white, they hide.
Stars above, like scattered lace,
Illuminate the frozen space.

Winds weave tales of ancient lore,
Through frosty wood and icy shore.
Each breath taken, a cloud's release,
In this realm, we find our peace.

The moon spills light on every scene,
Painting shadows, soft and keen.
In this shimmering, vast expanse,
Dreamers twirl in winter's dance.

Nebulae in a Winter's Grasp

In winter's hold, the skies ignite,
Nebulae swirl in celestial light.
Stars pulse softly, far and wide,
In cosmic realms where dreams abide.

Galaxies spin in frosty air,
Each glimmer weaving cosmic flair.
Whirling wonders, cold yet bright,
Carrying souls through starry night.

Veils of frost wrap all around,
In silence, beauty can be found.
Every spark, a story told,
Of ancient worlds and futures bold.

The void embraces, deep and vast,
A journey through the frozen past.
With every glance, the heart takes flight,
Nebulae dance in winter's light.

Winds of time, they softly call,
For wanderers lost within the thrall.
In this cold expanse, we see,
The universe's mystery.

The Frost-Touched Sky

Beneath a sky of azure hue,
Frost-kissed clouds drift softly through.
Whispers wrap the world in lace,
As winter's breath, we gently trace.

Stars emerge as daylight wanes,
In icy graces, love remains.
Each twinkle holds a tender sigh,
In the beauty of the frost-touched sky.

Luminous clouds, a silken cloak,
Where dreams take shape and voices croak.
The night unveils its velvet hue,
By cosmic light, we are renewed.

Frigid winds carry tales of peace,
In every corner, love finds lease.
A canvas painted with delight,
The frost-touched sky, a wondrous sight.

In serene moments, hearts align,
With every breath, the stars entwine.
Embracing all in purest grace,
In the stillness, we find our place.

Luminous Shivers Above

In shadows deep, a glow breaks free,
Luminous shivers call to me.
From every corner, spark and flare,
A vibrant dance fills icy air.

Softly flickering, the beams expand,
Guiding dreams with a gentle hand.
In each shimmer, a story spins,
Of frozen worlds where magic begins.

Snowflakes swirl like hidden charms,
Wrapped in whispers of winter's arms.
The night awakens with silver gleam,
In soft embrace, we chase the dream.

Above us, stars in joyous flight,
Raining down their shimmering light.
While the world sleeps in frosted peace,
The luminous shivers never cease.

Hearts aloft in the winter's night,
Bound together in gleaming light.
In the hush, our spirits soar,
Finding warmth forevermore.

Silence of Frozen Constellations

In the vastness, stars align,
Whispers lost in icy glow.
Time stands still, a breath divine,
As night's tapestry begins to grow.

Each flicker tells of ancient tales,
Secrets held in cosmic ice.
Underneath, the heart exhales,
Yearning for a taste of paradise.

Silence drapes like velvet night,
Chilling winds in gentle flow.
Beyond the void, a spark of light,
Guides the lost, the farthest soul.

Crystals twinkle from afar,
A dance upon the frozen sea.
Each moment shines, a fleeting star,
In the stillness, we are free.

Crystalline Nightfall

Among the trees, the shadows creep,
Moonlight weaves through every branch.
A tranquil dance, the world in sleep,
Where frosty dreams begin to prance.

Glimmering frost as wishes bloom,
Whispered secrets in the air.
A shimmering chill begins to loom,
Holding hope with tender care.

Stars adorn the velvet sky,
Glistening, like a lover's sigh.
Nightfall cradles, soft and sly,
Enchanting hearts, both low and high.

In silence rests the world anew,
A crystalline embrace of night.
Each heartbeat echoes, pure and true,
As dreams take flight, in moonlit flight.

Hushed Whispers of Comet Trails

Across the darkened, starry sea,
Comets streak with fleeting grace.
In their wake, a symphony,
Of whispers soft, they leave no trace.

Each glow a kiss upon the night,
A promise made, then lost in time.
Moments held in pure delight,
A cosmic dance, a fleeting rhyme.

Stardust drifts like dreams untold,
Carried far on winds so light.
In hushed tones, these tales unfold,
Crafting wonder in the night.

Echoes fade, still hearts remain,
Hushed whispers of a comet's flight.
Guiding souls through joy and pain,
Illuminating love's soft light.

Radiant Frost in Solitude

Alone beneath the frost-kissed trees,
Where silence holds its crystal breath.
Nature whispers through the breeze,
In solitude, we find our depth.

Each flake a gem, a fleeting thought,
Radiant dance in winter's heart.
Moments cherished, not forgot,
Painting dreams in frozen art.

As dawn breaks soft, the world awakes,
A canvas brushed with pale delight.
In solitude, the spirit shakes,
Finding peace in nature's light.

The world may spin, but here we stay,
Embraced by frost, the heart finds grace.
In radiant dawn, the shadows play,
And solitude, a warm embrace.

Twilight's Glacial Touch

In the quiet dusk light,
Shadows stretch and dance,
Colors blend and fade,
A fleeting, soft expanse.

Stars begin to shimmer,
Whispers in the breeze,
Coolness wraps around,
Like secrets in the trees.

Glacial glows upon the ground,
A world dressed in white,
Time seems to pause still,
In the calm of night.

Frozen breaths of winter,
Kissed by twilight's grace,
Moments linger softly,
In this sacred space.

Dreams drift like snowflakes,
In the dusk's embrace,
Each one holds a wish,
In twilight's glacial trace.

Ethereal Crystals of Space

Glistening in starlight,
Crystals hang so bright,
Floating through the cosmos,
In the velvet night.

Galaxies breathe softly,
Whirls of light appear,
Patterns intertwined,
Bringing dreams so near.

Ethereal whispers call,
From worlds yet unknown,
Mysteries of the night,
In the darkness shown.

Each fragment tells a tale,
Of time and distant place,
Interwoven stories,
In the void of space.

Crystals dance like fireflies,
In a cosmic thread,
Twinkling hopes alight,
In the starlit spread.

Luminescence in the Cold

Frosty air around me,
Shimmers in the dark,
A glow that softly breaks,
Winter's quiet spark.

Icicles like chandeliers,
Hanging from the eaves,
Each one catches light,
In the hush of leaves.

The moon casts silver rays,
On the icy ground,
Painting all in beauty,
Where serenity's found.

Luminous reflections,
Dance upon the frost,
Every flake a secret,
Of warmth that's never lost.

In this chill, I find warmth,
In the light so bold,
A place where dreams awaken,
In the luminescence of cold.

Frostbitten Wishes

The night wraps its arms tight,
In a blanket of white,
Chilled whispers ride the wind,
In the frosty night.

Each breath forms a crystal,
In the air so clear,
Wishes drift like snowflakes,
To the ground they steer.

Hope glimmers like ice shards,
In the moon's soft glow,
Promises of tomorrow,
In the silence flow.

With each star that twinkles,
A wish is set free,
Carried on the cold breeze,
Through the tall pine trees.

Nature holds my secrets,
In this winter's clutch,
Frostbitten wishes linger,
In the night's soft touch.

Frostbitten Beauty of Night's Canvas

A pale moon casts its glow,
Upon the shimmering snow,
Silent whispers grace the night,
In the stillness, dreams take flight.

Frosty tendrils kiss the trees,
Dancing softly with the breeze,
Each branch wears a crystal crown,
Nature dons her icy gown.

Stars awaken, twinkling bright,
Painting stories in the night,
Each spark a tale of old,
In the dark, their secrets told.

Night deepens, shadows blend,
Where the icy visions mend,
Colder hues embrace the air,
Whispers linger everywhere.

In this frozen, tranquil sight,
Beauty thrives in purest light,
Frostbitten dreams take their form,
Held within this winter's storm.

Lightyears Wrapped in Cold

Galaxies twinkle from afar,
Wrapped in blankets of cool starlight,
Lightyears stretch beyond the bold,
In this cosmic, frigid night.

Planets spin in silent grace,
Veils of frost across their face,
Time suspended, softly flows,
In this space where wonder grows.

Comets slice through velvet skies,
Trails of gleaming ice arise,
Adventures born in icy tail,
Echoing through the vast night's veil.

Nebulas, like frozen dreams,
Glitter quietly, so it seems,
In that hush, the universe,
Speaks in whispers, soft and terse.

Wrapped in cold, we drift and weave,
Among the stars, we dare believe,
In this stillness, hearts unfold,
In the mystery of the cold.

Echoing Whispers of Frozen Worlds

Beneath the frost, the silence hums,
As winter's breath quietly comes,
Echoes of worlds, both far and near,
Wrap us tightly, stark and clear.

Glaciers shimmer in moonlit haze,
Each crevice tells forgotten days,
Whispers curling in the chill,
Of stories time cannot kill.

Windswept valleys hold their breath,
Guardians of the frost and death,
Every flake a fleeting sound,
In these realms where peace is found.

Frozen rivers softly sigh,
Reflecting stars in midnight sky,
Journeying through the endless night,
Awakening dreams, pure and bright.

In this stillness, secrets dwell,
Time's embrace, a silent spell,
As echoes whisper through the frost,
In frozen worlds, we find the lost.

Stars in an Icy Lullaby

Cradled in the night so deep,
Stars sing soft, as shadows creep,
An icy lullaby so sweet,
Guiding dreams to find their feet.

Glinting gems on velvet cloth,
Whispers of the night's soft oath,
Every sparkle, a gentle wish,
In this moment, pure and brisk.

Frosted branches sway and glide,
Nature's beauty, snowflakes ride,
Breezes whisper through the trees,
Carrying tales on winter's ease.

Underneath the frosty dome,
Travelers find their way back home,
Through this quiet, starlit grace,
Finding warmth in winter's embrace.

In a dance of icy light,
Stars and dreams twirl through the night,
In this lullaby, soft and slow,
Hearts entwine in winter's glow.

Cascading Stardust

In the night, dreams take flight,
Whispers of stars, pure and bright.
Cascades shimmer, silver streams,
Weaving through our fleeting dreams.

Galaxies dance, a grand ballet,
Lost in wonders, hearts sway.
Each twinkle holds a secret plan,
In the cosmos' endless span.

Moonbeams twirl with gentle grace,
In this vast, enchanted space.
Cascading tales from far away,
With stardust, night turns to day.

Cosmic Chills and Silent Cries

In the void, cold winds blow,
Echoes linger, soft and slow.
Silent cries within the dark,
Finding warmth in a dim spark.

Stars hang low, brittle and frail,
Cosmic chills weave a quiet tale.
Galactic whispers, faint and clear,
Holding onto what we hear.

In the silence, depths appear,
Every heartbeat strays near.
Infinite space, a timeless sigh,
As we gaze at the endless sky.

Nocturnal Icicles of Light

Frosted whispers grace the night,
Icicles hang, jeweled and bright.
Each point reflects a glimmered song,
A symphony from the stars so long.

Glimmers dance on frozen streams,
Awakening the coldest dreams.
In crisp air, shadows entwine,
Nocturnal tales, a sacred sign.

Beneath the glow of a silver moon,
Icicles hum a gentle tune.
Fragile lights in winter's hold,
Eternal stories waiting to be told.

Dimensional Frost

In realms unseen, the frost gleams,
Woven in the fabric of dreams.
Dimensions blend in icy embrace,
Each flake a whisper, a timeless trace.

Crystalline paths of glimmering light,
Guide our souls through the endless night.
Frosty fingers stretch and tease,
Carving wonders with chilling breeze.

Through layers of time, we gently drift,
In a world where realities shift.
Frozen echoes, soft and vast,
Painting futures from the past.

Shivers Among the Astral Winds

In the night sky, shadows glide,
Whispers travel, no place to hide.
Stars flicker softly, a timeless song,
Among the winds, where shadows belong.

Chilled breath dances across the void,
Each moment fleeting, each glance enjoyed.
Hearts embrace the silence deep,
In cosmic realms, our secrets keep.

Ethereal lights weave through the dark,
Guiding lost souls with a gentle spark.
Underneath the celestial dome,
Shivers remind us we are not alone.

Galaxies spin in harmonies bright,
Echoes of love in the cold light.
Beneath the vastness, we find our place,
Cradled gently in the universe's embrace.

Together we wander, in awe we stand,
Hand in hand, through this radiant land.
With each shiver, a bond so sweet,
Among the astral winds, our hearts meet.

Hushed Radiance of the Starlit Fabric

Silken shadows weave through night,
Starlit whispers hold our sight.
Every twinkle, a tale untold,
In this fabric, dreams unfold.

Softly the universe draws us near,
In hush of stars, nothing to fear.
Infinite realms, the heart explores,
Beneath the gaze of cosmic shores.

Celestial rivers pulse and flow,
Guiding our steps where few dare go.
Veils of light, a tapestry spun,
In hushed radiance, we become one.

Glimmers of hope in the velvet skies,
Awakening wonder in weary eyes.
As night deepens, feelings bloom,
In this starlit fabric, we find home.

With every heartbeat, a promise dear,
In the hush of night, we hold near.
Radiance whispers, our spirits rise,
In the embrace of endless skies.

Borealis Whispers in Cosmic Chills

Across the sky, colors ignite,
Whispers of borealis paint the night.
In cosmic chills, the world stands still,
Nature's breath lingers, a tender thrill.

Green and gold in a frosty dance,
Lighting the heavens, as if by chance.
Waves of light in gentle sway,
Guiding our hearts on this winter's way.

Shivers race through starry strands,
Echoed soft in the ancient lands.
With every flicker, story flows,
In whispers of starlight, the magic grows.

Caught in the beauty, we close our eyes,
Beneath the spectacle of vibrant skies.
Together we cherish this timeless glow,
In borealis whispers, our spirits grow.

Cold winds carry a lullaby's grace,
Through cosmic chills, we find our place.
Underneath the northern light's thrill,
In the heart of winter, love's warmth still.

Starlight's Icy Caress

Under the dome, the night is clear,
Starlight's touch awakens sheer.
Icy elegance drapes the ground,
In its caress, solace is found.

Cold moon whispers secrets low,
Through cradled dreams, time does flow.
Each crystal flake, a story confined,
In starlight's grip, our fates entwined.

Frozen echoes point the way,
Through glimmers bright, we'll ever stay.
In the silence, hearts seek warmth,
In icy hands, a stoic charm.

Glistening pathways, stark and bright,
Breathe in the magic of the night.
With every shimmer, a promise stays,
In starlight's icy caress, we praise.

Together we wander, hand in hand,
Emerging in wonder, as dreams expand.
In this realm where cold winds flow,
Starlight's caress, forever aglow.

Celestial Rime and Radiance

Stars above in twilight's dance,
Whispers of a soft romance.
Moonlight drapes the world so bright,
Guiding dreams through velvet night.

Galaxies in shimmering hue,
Painting skies with shades so true.
Every sparkle, every gleam,
Holds the essence of a dream.

Breezes carry ancient tales,
Of cosmic winds and shooting trails.
Hearts entwined in astral flow,
Lost in wonders of the glow.

Time stands still in this embrace,
As we drift in endless space.
Moments linger, softly sway,
In the dance of night and day.

Whispers echo, secrets shared,
In the cosmos, love declared.
Celestial rime, sweet delight,
Awakens magic in the night.

Frostbitten Whispers Above

Frozen winds in silence roam,
Echoing the chill of home.
Stars are glimmering through the frost,
In this stillness, never lost.

Whispers of the icy night,
Painted skies, a wondrous sight.
Crystals shimmering from afar,
Telling tales of who we are.

Each breath visible in the air,
Moments felt beyond compare.
Time is frozen, hearts ablaze,
In this icy, starry haze.

Nature shimmers all around,
Beauty in the quiet found.
Frostbitten whispers brush the trees,
Swaying gently with the breeze.

In this realm, where dreams collide,
Hope ignites like stars that guide.
Frost-kissed nights hold endless art,
As the cosmos warms the heart.

A Universe Wrapped in Ice

A universe in glacial grace,
Draped in white, a cold embrace.
Each flake dances, soft and light,
In the glow of winter's night.

Mountains echo with the sound,
Of silence, beauty all around.
Crystals scatter, twinkling bright,
In the depths of starry night.

Frozen rivers, silvered dreams,
Reflecting moonlight's gentle beams.
Hearts are warmed by nature's care,
In this realm so rich and rare.

Winds of magic softly sigh,
As constellations roam the sky.
A universe wrapped in ice,
Where every moment feels so nice.

Glistening skies, a tranquil awe,
Holding wonders that leave us raw.
In this frozen, vast expanse,
We find joy in nature's dance.

Twinkling in a Cold Embrace

Stars are twinkling high above,
In the quiet, feels like love.
Snowflakes fall with gentle grace,
Kissing earth in cold embrace.

Moonlight bathes the world in silver,
Hearts awaken, shivers quiver.
Softly whispering through the night,
Guiding dreams in pure delight.

Reflecting on the icy streams,
Where whispers float and silence dreams.
Each moment holds a glowing spark,
In this timeless, wondrous dark.

Trees adorned with crystals bright,
Shimmer in the soft moonlight.
Winter's breath, a fleeting muse,
In a world we love to choose.

Twinkling stars, a symphony,
Composed in perfect harmony.
In this cold, we find our place,
Wrapped forever in its grace.

Ethereal Winter Scape

The snowflakes dance in twilight's glow,
Whispers of frost where cold winds blow.
Trees stand cloaked in silver arrays,
Nature's breath in quiet displays.

Stars above in a velvet sea,
Silent worlds call out to thee.
Moonlit paths of purest white,
Guiding souls through the gentle night.

Frozen rivers reflect the sky,
Mirrored dreams where spirits fly.
A frozen hush blankets the ground,
In this stillness, peace is found.

Wildlife traces soft in the snow,
Footprints vanish where cold winds blow.
The world wrapped tight in a crystal embrace,
Ethereal wonders in every space.

As dawn's light breaks, colors ignite,
A canvas shifts from dark to bright.
Winter's spell, a fleeting art,
A magic deep within the heart.

Cosmic Silence

In the void where stars align,
A silence drapes like velvet fine.
Galaxies twirl in gentle grace,
Lost in time, they find their place.

Whispers weave through cosmic night,
Echoes of long-forgotten light.
Darkness holds its breath in wait,
Entwined in the loom of fate.

Waves of silence gently flow,
Tides of time in endless glow.
Nebulas, painted in hues so rare,
Secrets float in the still, cold air.

Celestial wonders stretch and bend,
Infinite realms around the bend.
In the hush, new worlds take flight,
Crafting dreams from endless night.

Perception shifts beyond our sight,
In cosmic silence, we find our light.
To the stars, we drift and glide,
In the vastness, we confide.

Dreaming in Galactic Ice

In a dreamscape where glaciers gleam,
A tapestry woven from starlit theme.
Ice crystals catch the cosmic rays,
A world where time quietly sways.

Floating softly on frosted air,
Galactic whispers, beyond compare.
Nebulas bloom in colors bright,
Painting dreams in the still of night.

Each icy shard, a memory holds,
Stories in silence, ancient and bold.
Wonders drift under midnight skies,
In the realm where the frozen lies.

Stars sprinkle dust on tranquil seas,
Melodies dance like a gentle breeze.
Within this realm of icy lace,
We wander through the frozen space.

The cosmos wraps us in its charm,
No fears here, only warmth and calm.
Dreaming deep in this galactic peace,
In the stillness, all troubles cease.

A Chill from Beyond

From depths of space, a chill descends,
A cold that whispers, the heart it bends.
Mist from stars begins to rise,
Veils of breath, the essence of skies.

Shadows shift in the moonlight's grace,
In every corner, a haunting trace.
A frost that sings of worlds unseen,
Stories hidden where moonbeams glean.

With every gust, a secret shared,
Tales of journeys that none have dared.
The universe breathes a chilling thought,
Fragments of wonders forever caught.

In the night, silence reigns supreme,
Awakening dreams from a distant dream.
As frost etches its delicate art,
A chill from beyond whispers in heart.

In the stillness, we seek sign,
Caught in the web of the cosmic design.
The chill from beyond, a sacred thread,
Binding the living with the dead.

Shadows of a Frozen Galaxy

In the silence deep and vast,
Shadows linger, memories cast.
Frozen whispers dance in night,
A galaxy cloaked in dim light.

Stars hang like stories untold,
Each one a dream, brave and bold.
Twinkling jewels in darkened skies,
Eternal echoes, soft goodbyes.

Beneath the shimmer, secrets lie,
Silent shadows drift and sigh.
Time flows like a river of frost,
In the stillness, we find what's lost.

Navigating through the chill,
Wandering souls, we seek our fill.
Amongst the shadows, we query,
The frozen galaxy whispers, "Hurry."

Yet, in this hush, we feel alive,
Each heartbeat, a spark to survive.
Through the shadows, we break free,
In the galaxy, we find our key.

Aurora's Subtle Breath

In the dawn's embrace, colors swirl,
An aurora's breath begins to unfurl.
Gentle hues, soft and light,
Chasing away remnants of night.

A dance across the silent sky,
Whispering secrets, as they fly.
Colors woven in fleeting grace,
Awakening dreams, a warm embrace.

Through valleys deep, the light cascades,
Nature's canvas, where stillness fades.
Beneath the glow, shadows retreat,
Filling the world with radiant heat.

Each flicker sings of the rebirth,
A soft reminder of the earth.
In the quiet, we pause and stare,
At the beauty that lingers in the air.

Boundless wonders swirl above,
A tapestry stitched with love.
Aurora's breath, subtle and bright,
Guiding us gently into the light.

Crystalline Dreams Among the Stars

In the night, dreams crystallize,
Drifting softly through the skies.
Stars appear like scattered gems,
Whispers of love in their diadems.

Among the glimmers, visions gleam,
Reality fades, as we dream.
Each twinkling light, a wish we make,
In the vastness, our spirits wake.

Crystalline forms take shape and rise,
Translucent hopes in cosmic ties.
A symphony of starlit views,
Painting the night with shades of blues.

We chase the echoes of the past,
In this expanse, our hearts hold fast.
Through the cosmos, we gently roam,
Finding solace, a place called home.

Among the constellations, we weave,
Crystalline dreams, we dare believe.
In the embrace of endless night,
Stars guide our journey towards the light.

Glittering Light on a Frozen Sea

On the surface, crystal gleams,
A frozen sea with shattered dreams.
Light dances on the icy crest,
Whispers of stories left unguessed.

Waves of silence, a tranquil flow,
Reflecting stars in the midnight glow.
Each glimmer tells a tale untold,
Of sailors lost, and hearts made bold.

Beneath, the depths hold secrets tight,
In the dark, lies the true plight.
But the surface sparkles, a gentle tease,
Crafting illusions upon the freeze.

As we walk, our thoughts intertwine,
With the beauty of the sea that shines.
In the stillness, we pause and see,
The glittering light, how it sets us free.

On this frozen sea, we dare to dream,
Catching reflections of light, a beam.
Glittering whispers call us near,
In the silence, we conquer fear.

Whispers of Celestial Frost

In the stillness, whispers flow,
Under moonlight's gentle glow.
Crystals sparkle in the breeze,
Nature's breath, a silent tease.

Echoes dance on winter's air,
Softly wrapped in silver glare.
Mysteries of the night unfold,
Tales of warmth in the cold.

Stars above in icy flight,
Guiding dreams through frosty night.
Each glimmer a soft kiss,
A moment wrapped in bliss.

Beneath blankets of pure white,
Whispers weave in darkened light.
A silent world, so serene,
In this frost, we commune.

Through the shadows, secrets glide,
In the hush, the heart confides.
Whispers from the cosmic sea,
Embrace all that's yet to be.

Nightfall's Icy Embrace

As day departs, the chill descends,
Wrapping all in icy bends.
The sky blushes in twilight's hold,
A tale of night in darkness told.

Underneath a silken shroud,
Dreams emerge from shadows loud.
Each breath a fog, each sigh a mist,
In winter's grasp, we exist.

Stars emerge with gentle grace,
As nightfall weaves its silent lace.
A cold kiss upon the cheek,
In dreams, the heart finds what it seeks.

The world sleeps in a frozen trance,
Caught in winter's timeless dance.
Crystals form where echoes soar,
Night's embrace forevermore.

In the hush, the whispers flow,
Secrets only the night may know.
Wrapped in frost, we softly dream,
In the nightfall's icy theme.

Starlit Frigid Veil

Beneath the stars, a canvas bright,
Painted in the coldest light.
A veil of frost, a glimmering sheet,
Whispers of winter beneath our feet.

Each twinkling gem, a wish untold,
Enticing tales from ages old.
In the silence, time stands still,
The night's embrace, a tranquil thrill.

Through the chill, a soft refrain,
Echoes linger in the lane.
Breezes carry secrets far,
Guided by a silent star.

Wrapped in veils of icy grace,
In every corner, nature's face.
A world adorned in silver hues,
Beneath the sky, a tranquil muse.

Moments still in starlit glow,
Each breath a crystal, pure as snow.
In this realm, hearts intertwine,
Underneath the celestial sign.

Frozen Echoes in the Cosmos

In the void where silence reigns,
Frozen echoes mark the plains.
Stars like diamonds, cold and bright,
Whisper tales of the endless night.

A cosmic dance in frosty air,
Timeless secrets everywhere.
Within the dark, a melody sings,
Carried forth on winter's wings.

Galaxies wrapped in frigid bows,
Mysteries linger, nobody knows.
Through the depths of icy seas,
The universe whispers with ease.

In the shadows, dreams arise,
Shimmering truths in starry skies.
Frozen echoes, soft and clear,
Resonate in the stillness near.

Each heartbeat syncs with cosmic tides,
In the chill where magic hides.
Captured in this tranquil space,
Frozen echoes, time's embrace.

Nightfall's Frigid Embrace

As shadows stretch across the land,
The chill descends, a tender hand.
Stars awaken, bright and clear,
Embracing night, dissolving fear.

Whispers ride the icy breeze,
Nature sighs, the world at ease.
Moonlight dances on the ground,
Crickets sing, a soothing sound.

A blanket woven, dark and deep,
Inviting dreams, in silence steep.
Cool breath flows through every tree,
Nightfall's song, a symphony.

In the dark, there lies a glow,
The tranquil heart of night's soft show.
Time suspends, a gentle pause,
In frigid grasp, we find its cause.

Awake, the world in quiet grace,
Held firm in night's frigid embrace.
Each heartbeat echoes, slow and true,
Beneath the stars, our spirits grew.

Celestial Coolness

In the cosmos, coolness reigns,
Stars like diamonds, no refrains.
Galaxies swirl in velvet black,
Whispering secrets, no turning back.

The moon a guardian, bold and bright,
Bathing us in gentle light.
Comets rush, with tails aflame,
Celestial coolness, no two the same.

Nebulas paint the skies anew,
With every hue, a vibrant view.
Frozen stardust, drifting wide,
The universe, our cosmic guide.

Echoes of ages lost in time,
Celestial rhythms, a silent rhyme.
Every breath, a breath of space,
Coolness ignites, a soft embrace.

To witness such, a dazzling show,
In the vastness, peace does flow.
Celestial coolness, eternal sway,
In night's embrace, we drift away.

Frozen Echoes of the Universe

In the distance, echoes ring,
Frozen whispers softly cling.
Voices drift through cosmic trails,
In silence deep, the heart prevails.

Stars murmuring in ancient lore,
Light-years travel, forevermore.
Each spark holds stories left untold,
Frozen echoes, brave and bold.

Nebulas sigh, a shimmering veil,
Crystalline fragments tell the tale.
Galaxies spin, entwined with grace,
In frozen realms, we find our place.

The universe, a canvas wide,
With every echo, secrets hide.
Mysteries wrapped in cosmic frost,
In twilight's grip, we find what's lost.

Moments captured, soft and bright,
Frozen echoes, a guiding light.
In this vast, eternal night,
We wander through the starry sight.

Galactic Shivers

Underneath an endless sky,
Galactic shivers pass us by.
Planets twirl in silent spheres,
Whispers carried through the years.

Cosmic winds caress our skin,
In the depths, a world within.
Starry fields, a vast expanse,
Each glance draws us, a trance-like dance.

Distant worlds, we dream to find,
Galactic shivers, hearts entwined.
Wonders beckon from afar,
Chasing light, we follow stars.

Nebulae breathe in shades of gold,
Timeless tales in starlight told.
Each flicker, a petal's fall,
In twilight's grip, we heed the call.

Galaxies swirl, a painted night,
In our souls, we feel the light.
Beyond the void, where silence lives,
Galactic shivers, the night forgives.

Beneath the Stellar Gaze

Stars whisper secrets in the night,
A tapestry of pure delight.
Dreams take flight on silver beams,
Lost in the dance of cosmic dreams.

The moon hangs low, a ghostly sight,
Illuminating shadows with its light.
In silence, we share our fears,
The universe listens, it hears.

With each heartbeat, we feel the trace,
Of ancient echoes in this place.
Galaxies swirl, a vibrant play,
We're but stardust underneath their sway.

Comets streak across the vast expanse,
Nature's wonders in a cosmic dance.
Together we breathe, hearts align,
Beneath the stars, your hand in mine.

A fleeting moment, the world's a stage,
Caught in the spell of the stellar gaze.
Let's linger here, forever stay,
And paint our dreams in the Milky Way.

Icy Dreams of Distant Worlds

In the silence of the night, I see,
Icy dreams call out to me.
Whispers from stars that shine so bright,
Tales of worlds in frozen flight.

Snowflakes drift on the cosmic breeze,
Melting hearts under moonlit trees.
Galaxies twinkle in cold embrace,
Time stands still in this sacred space.

Comets trail with a frosty plume,
Guiding lost souls through the gloom.
Distant worlds, in a chilling glow,
Awaiting the dreams we dare not show.

Crystals shimmer on a silver sea,
Each reflection a memory.
Icy visions, dreams unfold,
In the cosmos, a story told.

As the night deepens, we take flight,
On icy dreams into the night.
With each breath, we break the mold,
In distant worlds, our hearts turn bold.

Breath of the Night Sky

The night sky breathes, a gentle sigh,
Stars flutter like wings, oh so high.
In the velvet dark, secrets blend,
Whispers of time that never end.

A canvas painted with cosmic hues,
Endless stories await to muse.
Each twinkle a promise, hope alight,
Guiding the lost through the night.

Moonbeams kiss the tranquil earth,
Glimmers of magic, infinite worth.
Embraced by shadows, we find our way,
In the breath of the night, we sway.

Constellations weave a knitted dream,
Navigating hearts like a soft stream.
With each sigh, we reach for more,
In the night sky's breath, we soar.

Infinite wonders, a timeless dance,
Under the heavens, we take our chance.
With stardust wishes, hearts entwine,
In the night's embrace, forever shine.

Frost on the Milky Way

Frosty petals on the Milky Way,
Whispering tales of yesterday.
Each crystal, a fragment intertwined,
Stories of love, gently outlined.

Galaxies swirl in the cold night air,
Time seems to pause, a moment rare.
Frozen light beams, softly aglow,
Guiding our paths where dreams may flow.

With every heartbeat, the cosmos hums,
Echoes of time, the universe drums.
Step by step on this frosty trail,
We chase the echoes, we dance, we sail.

As we wander through the frost-kissed skies,
Under the wonder, the heart complies.
Cold kisses warm under stardust rays,
In the shimmer and glow of our days.

Let's trace our fingers on the starlit sea,
In the frost of dreaming, just you and me.
With every breath, our souls align,
On the Milky Way, eternally shine.

Celestial Crystals in Midnight Air

In the silence of the night,
Crystals glimmer with pure light.
Each star a whispered secret,
Floating in the soft moon's bite.

Gentle breezes brush the ground,
A symphony of dreams resound.
Echoes of a world untold,
In the darkness, magic found.

Shadows dance with silver gleam,
Time unfolds like a delicate dream.
Wonders spark in starlit skies,
Where the heart learns to believe.

Nature's palette, bold and bright,
Painting love in colors light.
Celestial whispers, soft and sweet,
In midnight air, our souls take flight.

Through the crystals, stories flow,
Of distant lands, of ebb and flow.
In each shard, a tale resides,
Where imagination dares to go.

Glacial Luminance and Shattered Dreams

In the realm of ice and snow,
Shattered dreams begin to glow.
Glacial blooms of frozen light,
Whisper tales of winter's plight.

Beneath the surface, still and cold,
Lie ambitions bright and bold.
Each shard reflects a wish once dreamed,
In the vastness, hopes redeemed.

Winds of change both fierce and free,
Carve the landscape patiently.
In the breath of frost and air,
Lies the strength to start anew.

Luminance in quiet nights,
Guiding lost, forgotten sprites.
Turn the darkness into light,
With every single fading sight.

Mountains loom, their majesty,
Guardians of our history.
Feel the chill of broken dreams,
Glacial whispers softly gleam.

Sapient Stars in Frozen Ether

Stars awaken with ancient minds,
In the ether, wisdom finds.
Frozen realms where thoughts roam free,
Celestial guides for you and me.

Each twinkle holds a mystery,
A dance of fate and destiny.
The cosmos speaks with gentle grace,
Embracing all in its warm embrace.

From the depths of night's expanse,
Sapient dreams begin to dance.
Every heartbeat in the dark,
Each pulse a starlit spark.

In this vast and endless sea,
Love and hope entwined to be.
Through the silent, frozen air,
Truth emerges, pure and rare.

Gather wisdom from the skies,
See the world through loving eyes.
As stars sing their timeless tune,
We find our light; we find our moon.

Elysian Frost Beneath Cosmic Veils

Elysium beneath the dark,
Frosted whispers, nature's spark.
Cosmic veils of shimmering night,
Wrap the world in soft twilight.

Each flake a wish that soars and glides,
Over landscapes where hope resides.
Underneath the crystal skies,
Dreams awaken, never die.

In the stillness, hearts entwined,
Secrets of the universe aligned.
Beneath the frost, a warmth so deep,
In the quiet, love we keep.

Every breath, a sacred song,
Echoes where we all belong.
Here in twilight's gentle fold,
Stories of our lives unfold.

Elysian lands invite all souls,
To seek wholeness, to feel whole.
Through cosmic veils, we share our fate,
Embracing light, it's never too late.

Chill of the Infinite Night

Stars whisper softly in dark skies,
Moonlight dances where silence lies.
Dreams drift gently on the breeze,
Wrapped in shadows, time now flees.

Cold winds carry tales untold,
Of ancient worlds, both dark and bold.
Infinity hums a lullaby sweet,
As night unfolds its calming sheet.

The universe breathes in deep sighs,
While galaxies spin and softly rise.
In the vastness, we find a spark,
Guiding us gently through the dark.

Each twinkling light a distant friend,
Whispers of hope in the night extend.
Wrapped in the chill of woven dreams,
Life is more than what it seems.

Embrace the peace, the cosmic flight,
In the beauty of the infinite night.
Hold your breath with wonder anew,
As the heavens cast their view.

Frosty Veils of Dream

Under a blanket of silver gleam,
Lonely whispers fill the dream.
Frosty veils of shimmering light,
Bathe the world in cold delight.

Snowflakes twirl in a playful ballet,
Each one unique in its soft display.
They paint the earth in a crystal hue,
An enchanting scene, serene and true.

Silence blankets the earth's embrace,
Every step leaves a fragile trace.
In this realm where time stands still,
Hearts awaken from winter's chill.

Dreamers wander on paths of white,
Lost in the beauty of endless night.
With frosty breath, we weave our tales,
Chasing shadows where wonder prevails.

Embroidering hope in the icy air,
In frosty veils, we find our care.
Each moment a memory, softly formed,
In the quiet, our hearts are warmed.

Celestial Fingerprints in Ice

In the stillness, time carves its path,
Celestial footprints in a crystal bath.
The heavens trace their ancient art,
While ice reflects the sky's own heart.

Fractals dance on the frozen glass,
Whispers of starlight, fleeting, pass.
Each pattern tells a story untold,
Of cosmic wonders, beautiful and bold.

Galaxies swirl in a frozen embrace,
With icy fingers that leave no trace.
In the tapestry of night, they weave,
An unending tale for those who believe.

The chill penetrates the soul's deep core,
Sparks of magic in the shadowed fore.
Every breath a connection to the skies,
With celestial fingerprints, the spirit flies.

Embrace the silence, let dreams ignite,
In celestial fingerprints of the night.
Hold the wonder of the frozen scene,
Where ice and stars create the serene.

Chilled Emotions from the Cosmos

Whispers echo through the cosmic wide,
Chilled emotions in the universe hide.
A tapestry woven with dreams and fears,
Starlit memories, shedding soft tears.

Amongst the stars, our stories blend,
Where time and space curiously bend.
Frozen sighs hold secrets deep,
In the depths of the slumbering sleep.

In the shadows where feelings roam,
The chill of night feels like home.
Each heartbeat syncs with the galactic flow,
As the cosmos echoes the things we know.

Falling softly like the world's embrace,
Chilled emotions find their place.
With every glance at the vast expanse,
We yield our souls to the cosmic dance.

From the ether, where thoughts ignite,
Chilled emotions take their flight.
In the still of night, our spirits soar,
Connect to the cosmos forevermore.

Frigid Echoes of Time Past

In the silence where shadows creep,
Memories linger, secrets keep.
Whispers echo through the cold,
Stories of love and loss retold.

Beneath the frost, time seems to freeze,
In every sigh, a gentle breeze.
Eons pass with a subtle grace,
Leaving only a ghostly trace.

Snowflakes dance in the pale moonlight,
As echoes fade into the night.
Each step taken on frozen ground,
Resonates with the thoughts unbound.

Through the haze where the past resides,
In winter's arms, the heart confides.
Endless moments lost in the dim,
Frigid echoes, the past's whim.

Yet in each chill, a warmth remains,
A glimmer caught in frozen chains.
Time may fade, but memories last,
In frigid echoes of time past.

Shimmers of Icy Elysium

In realms where starlight softly glows,
The ice reflects what nature knows.
Veils of crystal touch the night,
As shimmers weave in pure delight.

Fragrant winds carry dreams untold,
Through glades of silver, crisp and bold.
Each breath mingles with the serene,
In icy vistas, pure and clean.

Dancing lights on a frozen lake,
Whisper secrets, choices we make.
Elysium wrapped in a frosty shell,
Where echoes linger, and spirits dwell.

Frozen branches cradle the stars,
A gentle beauty, without scars.
Each shiver breathes a timeless art,
A canvas painted straight from the heart.

In this world of glistening light,
Hopes are born in the chilly night.
Shimmers glow in a tranquil view,
Portraying dreams that feel anew.

Tranquility Frosted

Amidst the snow, a quiet hush,
Nature pauses in a gentle rush.
Frost blankets all in silence deep,
While weary hearts find peace in sleep.

The world transformed in white so pure,
A tranquil calm, a soothing cure.
Winds whisper soft through barren trees,
Carrying notes of winter's peace.

Footprints trace paths in glistening snow,
A solitary journey, quiet and slow.
In the cool embrace, time stands still,
Reflecting the heart's own sacred will.

Each flake that falls, a lost refrain,
Tales of joy, and echoes of pain.
Yet in this frosted realm we find,
A solace born from nature's kind.

As twilight fades, a stillness reigns,
Under soft glows, the darkness wanes.
Tranquility wrapped in a winter's shroud,
Invites the soul to feel unbowed.

Aether's Shivering Veil

In twilight's grasp, the world suspended,
The aether wraps, softly blended.
Shimmers dance upon the breeze,
A veil of dreams that seeks to please.

Each star a whisper from the night,
Casting shadows, lending light.
In this realm where visions play,
The heart unfolds, leading the way.

Glistening paths in the cosmic flow,
Unravel where we long to go.
A shivering touch from the sky above,
Connecting all with threads of love.

In moments held between each breath,
We ponder life and dance with death.
Yet in the aether's woven thread,
Hope rises, inviting the led.

A realm where time swirls, undefined,
Beckoning thoughts to intertwine.
Aether's veil, where dreams unveil,
Whispers of the universe, we inhale.

Glacial Serenade Underneath the Void

In the cradle of ice, whispers dwell,
Softly singing tales no one can tell.
Stars hang low, like dreams that float,
Chilling visions in a silver boat.

Snowflakes dance on a midnight breeze,
Painting silence with frosty ease.
The moon's glimmer guides the way,
Through this wonderland where shadows sway.

Beneath the dark, the world holds breath,
Nestled close, yet bound to death.
Crystals shimmer with ancient lore,
Echoing secrets from days of yore.

Icicles form in a frozen symphony,
Nature's whisper, a solemn decree.
In every flake, a history clear,
Sings of longing, of love, and fear.

Awakening dreams in the still of night,
Glacial serenade, a haunting sight.
In the void, where silence reigns,
Melodies linger, like whispered chains.

Frozen Light Across the Cosmos

In the midnight sky, stars gleam bright,
A whisper of dreams in the pale moonlight.
Galaxies swirl in the stillness above,
A dance of the cosmos, a tale of love.

Comets streak past, with tails made of fire,
Chasing the echoes of a deep desire.
Nebulae glow in colors so bold,
Stories of ages and wonders untold.

Frozen light travels through the expanse,
In cosmic silence, the galaxies dance.
Each flicker recalls a time long gone,
A symphony played on the strings of dawn.

Endless horizons in darkness unfold,
The secrets of space in their grasp, they hold.
In the realm of stars, where the shadows play,
Hope sows its seed in the light of the day.

Lost in the lift of the endless night,
We find our way guided by frozen light.
Across the vastness, a journey begins,
In the heart of darkness, the solace it brings.

Frigid Echoes of Celestial Lyric

In the realm where cold winds sigh,
Frigid echoes of nights gone by.
Celestial whispers, soft and clear,
Carrying dreams wrapped in sheer fear.

Waves of starlight gently collide,
With memories that time cannot hide.
The pulse of the cosmos flows through space,
In the stillness, we find our place.

A tapestry woven from night's own breath,
Haunted by specters of life and death.
Each crystal note, a song in the dark,
Guiding lost souls towards a spark.

In this vast silence, stories unfold,
Bold and delicate, treasured yet cold.
Every echo a piece of the night,
Holding the key to our inner light.

Frigid whispers, lift us high,
To realms beyond where the spirits fly.
In the embrace of the cosmic sea,
We find the lyrics that set us free.

Sparkling Gaze of the Silent Night

Amidst the glow of the starlit sky,
A tranquil hush, where shadows lie.
Whispers of dreams in the velvet air,
Hold the secrets that night can share.

Sparkles twinkle, like a thousand souls,
In the stillness, where the universe rolls.
Hearts beat softly to a cosmic tune,
Under the watch of a silvery moon.

Frosty breath hangs in the chilling night,
Painting our moments with crystal light.
In the gleam of the darkness, we trace our fate,
Finding solace in this timeless state.

Each twinkle calls, a silent refrain,
Bringing forth joy, wrapped in the pain.
From depths of silence, strength does rise,
In sparkling gazes, past midnight skies.

Together we wander, hand in hand,
Through the frozen grasp of this enchanted land.
In the embrace of the night's gentle plea,
We uncover truths, just you and me.

Frost-Laden Memories in Distant Light

Frost-kissed mornings bring back to mind,
Echoes of laughter, gentle and kind.
Memories wrapped in a blanket of white,
Glowing softly in the gathering light.

Each crystal holds the stories we made,
Moments captured, never to fade.
In the glimmer of dawn, they come alive,
Dancing in shadows, where dreams survive.

Time drips slowly from branches bare,
Whispers of frost, woven with care.
In the flicker of light, we find our way,
Back to the warmth of a golden day.

With every step on this frozen floor,
I hear the echoes of love we swore.
In the chill of the air, I can still sense,
The warmth of your smile, a sweet recompense.

As the sun rises, painting the scene,
Frost-laden memories weave through the serene.
In the distance, a glimpse of what's right,
Fleeting moments in radiant light.

Stellar Winter

In the chill of the night, the universe sleeps,
Blanketed softly, as silence creeps.
Stars like snowflakes, each one unique,
Whispers of winter, so calm and meek.

Frozen winds carry a cosmic tune,
Echoes of starlight, beneath the moon.
Constellations shimmer, a frosty embrace,
A tapestry woven in celestial grace.

Comets glide by with a shimmering tail,
Stories of journeys through time they unveil.
A universe cloaked in a soft, white haze,
Wonders of winter set hearts all ablaze.

The cosmos breathes in the still of the dark,
A canvas painted with each distant spark.
In this stellar winter, beauty is found,
As silence blankets the vastness around.

In crystal-clear nights, our dreams take flight,
We dance in the glow of the stars' pure light.
In the heart of winter, we find our way,
Guided by stardust till dawn of the day.

Glistening Aether

In the depths of night, the aether sways,
Glistening softly in a million ways.
The cosmos echoes with radiant grace,
Each star, a story, a luminous trace.

Waves of light in a celestial sea,
Reflect the wonders of what could be.
In the quiet moments of cosmic flow,
The heart of the universe starts to glow.

Glistening brilliance, a dance of delight,
Painted in colors that banish the night.
Constellations weave through the fabric of time,
Crafting a rhythm, a celestial rhyme.

Through the layers of space, the light draws near,
Filling the void with a warmth so dear.
A tapestry bright where the spirits roam,
In the heart of the aether, we find our home.

Each twinkle a wish whispered to the sky,
A glimmer of hope that will never die.
In the vast expanse, our dreams take flight,
In the embrace of the glistening light.

Chilling Radiance

A chilling glow in the depths of the night,
Radiance flickers, an ethereal light.
Frozen horizons stretch far and wide,
In the hush of the dark, where secrets hide.

Celestial whispers ride on the breeze,
Carrying tales from the stars with ease.
Light dances softly, a ghostly ballet,
In the cold of the cosmos, it finds its way.

Illuminated paths through the shadows weave,
Offering solace to those who believe.
The chill of the night wraps the world in grace,
As the chilling radiance bathes every space.

Colors that shimmer in brilliant design,
Across the expanse, a celestial line.
Each flicker of light tells a story profound,
In the silence of winter, our hearts pound.

With every heartbeat, the night comes alive,
In the chilling radiance, our spirits thrive.
Echoes of starlight stretch far and clear,
Guiding our dreams through the atmosphere.

Radiant Frost and Shimmering Light

In the dawn's gentle embrace,
Radiant frost glistens bright,
Whispers of winter's soft grace,
Shimmering beams dance with delight.

Crystals weave a delicate lace,
Nature's art in morning's sight,
Each breath a fleeting trace,
Of warmth amidst the chill of night.

Bare branches cloaked in snow,
Silent sentinels of the cold,
Underneath the winter's glow,
Stories of the brave and bold.

As sunrays chase the shadows wide,
Frozen tears begin to thaw,
In the heart where dreams abide,
Hope emerges with a thaw.

Radiant frost, a fleeting show,
Transcending time, it's pure delight,
In a world where soft winds blow,
Shimmering light in endless flight.

Evening's Frosted Horizon

The sun dips low, a golden kiss,
Evening's frost begins to rise,
A tranquil spell, a moment's bliss,
Wrapped beneath the twilight skies.

Winds whisper tales of love once lost,
Carried on the sighs of night,
In the chill, we feel the cost,
Of dreams that vanish out of sight.

Frosted fields in silver hue,
Stars begin to twinkle bright,
In the hush, the world feels new,
Beneath the cloak of fading light.

As shadows stretch across the land,
Hope flickers in each frozen breath,
Together here, we bravely stand,
Embracing beauty even in death.

Evening wraps the earth in grace,
Frosted whispers fill the space,
In the heart, we find our place,
Quiet peace, a warm embrace.

Constellations in a Breath of Frost

Stars emerge like diamonds bright,
Constellations hanging low,
A breath of frost, a magical sight,
Glistening softly, in the glow.

Each twinkle tells a frozen tale,
Of nights where dreams come alive,
In the silence, air grows pale,
With every wish, the hopes survive.

Moonlit paths of silver thread,
Lead us through the icy night,
Where stories of the brave are spread,
In a dance of shadowed light.

With every sigh, the chill ignites,
A spark of warmth within our hearts,
As constellations fill the heights,
Reminding us how nature imparts.

In a breath of frost, we dream,
Stars align in cosmic grace,
Together we, a radiant beam,
Wheel of fate in time and space.

Diaspora of Cold Starlight

From winter's grasp, we rise anew,
A diaspora of cold starlight,
Chasing shadows into the blue,
Embraced by night's eternal flight.

Each glimmer sings a distant song,
Of worlds untraveled yet to see,
With every heartbeat, we belong,
In the fabric of infinity.

Cold winds carry dreams away,
On sparkling wings, they soar high,
In this journey, we find our way,
Underneath the vast, dark sky.

The universe in frozen dance,
Whirls of light across our path,
An invitation to take a chance,
To learn, to love, to feel the math.

In a diaspora of cold starlight,
We are the whispers of the night,
Born of frost, we spark the flight,
Together, shining ever bright.

Astral Frost Lace

In the stillness of the night,
Whispers of the stars take flight.
Draped in frost, the world awakes,
A tapestry that heaven makes.

Glittering strands weave in the dark,
Where silence sings, and illusions spark.
Each flake a dream, a story spun,
Under the gaze of the midnight sun.

Chasing echoes of a lost embrace,
The moon adorns this frozen space.
With every breath, the cosmos breathes,
In frosted lace, the heart believes.

Glimmers dance upon the snow,
As light and shadow play below.
Nature's art, a fleeting show,
In winter's depth, we find our glow.

Awakening in this quiet scene,
An astral beauty, serene and keen.
With every step the world unfolds,
In astral frost, our dreams are told.

Solidity in the Ether

Between the stars where shadows cling,
Lies an essence, a quiet spring.
Matter woven in ethereal threads,
Where every thought and moment spreads.

Particles dance in cosmic embrace,
Forming worlds in infinite space.
A solid truth in dreams we chase,
Navigating through time's gentle pace.

Gravity pulls in a soft refrain,
Binding us close in joy and pain.
In the ether, our spirits soar,
Finding warmth on this cosmic shore.

The essence of stars in a single gaze,
Ignites the mind in a brilliant blaze.
Solidity formed from intangible grace,
In the depths of night, we carve our place.

With every heartbeat, we pulse and flow,
Through the dark beyond, to the light we go.
A journey of souls through the cosmos vast,
In the solidity of the ether, we last.

Celestial Winter's Night

Underneath a quilt of dark,
The universe leaves its mark.
Frozen whispers fill the air,
As dreams alight on winter's glare.

Shooting stars where heavens meet,
Celestial wonders feel so sweet.
In the quiet of the snowy scene,
Magic glimmers, pure and clean.

Icicles hang like crystal spears,
Holding close the night-time fears.
Yet in their beauty lies a balm,
A tranquil hush, a soothing calm.

With every breath, we taste the chill,
As time slows down, and spirits thrill.
Under starlit skies, hearts ignite,
In the stillness of the winter's night.

Touched by frost, we feel alive,
In the celestial dance, we strive.
Each moment spells its own delight,
A symphony, celestial winter's night.

Glimmering Ice of Distant Galaxies

Beyond the hills where shadows freeze,
Lies a realm that knows no ease.
Glimmering ice, a cosmic sea,
Where galaxies drift, wild and free.

In the quiet, the silence sings,
Of infinite realms and ancient things.
Stars like diamonds, bright and rare,
Reflect the dreams we all must share.

The cold embrace of space invites,
Journeys long into starry nights.
With every step on this frosted ground,
Echoes of creation can be found.

Crystals shimmer, cosmic art,
Melding worlds that won't depart.
Through the void, we feel the lure,
Of distant galaxies, vast and pure.

In the glimmer, our souls ignite,
As we dance through the endless night.
Glimmering ice, a sight divine,
In the heart of space, our fates align.

Chilling Nightscapes

Stars flicker in the dark,
Whispers brush the silent park.
Moonlight dances on the trees,
A haunting tune carried by the breeze.

Shadows stretch across the ground,
In this solitude, peace is found.
Chill seeps in, a gentle sigh,
As night unfolds its velvet sky.

Frost glistens on every blade,
Each step taken is softly made.
The world slumbers, wrapped in dreams,
Where nothing's ever as it seems.

Winter whispers secrets low,
In this realm, where cold winds blow.
Every breath creates a fog,
As I wander through this bog.

The horizon blends night and day,
Where light and shadow tend to play.
Chilling nightscapes hold the key,
To a world where spirits roam free.

Ethereal Cold

A whisper of frost in the air,
An ethereal touch, subtle and rare.
Silvery dreams swirl all around,
In this cold embrace, warmth is found.

Stars are jewels in the midnight's veil,
Their twinkling lights tell an ancient tale.
The silence sings a haunting song,
In this beauty where I belong.

Each breath fogs like a fleeting ghost,
In this winter realm, I linger the most.
Winds weave stories through the night,
A tapestry spun with sheer delight.

Moonbeams cradle the sleeping earth,
As night unveils its hidden worth.
Ethereal whispers kiss my skin,
Inviting dreams that draw me in.

The frost-laden branches sway with grace,
In the twilight hour, I find my place.
A tranquil hush envelops my soul,
In this ethereal scene, I feel whole.

Luminous Frigid Horizons

The dawn breaks with a shimmering light,
Casting jewels across the night.
Luminous hues paint the skies,
As the day awakens with soft sighs.

Frigid winds in a gentle sweep,
Awaken the world from its sleepy keep.
Shadows dance on the crystal snow,
In this radiant, frosty glow.

Horizon stretches far and wide,
Where icy breaths and dreams collide.
Sunrise spills gold on icy lakes,
As nature stirs and softly wakes.

Each moment glistens, time stands still,
Chasing echoes on the frosty hill.
Luminous whispers ride the breeze,
Creating visions with perfect ease.

The world anew beneath the sun,
Cascading colors, the day's begun.
Luminous frigid horizons shine,
A reminder of nature's divine.

Glacial Glimmers of Time

Time drifts slowly, like falling snow,
Each moment a glacial, gentle show.
Memories frozen in crystal clear,
Echoes of laughter, whispers of fear.

In this winter realm, thoughts unwind,
Woven in silence, the heart's kind.
Glimmers of light pierce through the gloom,
Highlighting the beauty of winter's bloom.

Frosty images flash in my mind,
In the depth of winter, peace I find.
Life slows down with each frosty breath,
In this dance with shadows of death.

A canvas of ice where dreams may roam,
In the heart of the cold, we find our home.
Glacial glimmers, soft and bright,
Mark the passage of day and night.

Each spark a reminder of times gone by,
In the stillness, our spirits fly.
Glacial glimmers of time unfold,
In the icy grasp, stories are told.

Frosty Glimmers Through the Cosmic Gaze

In the stillness of the night,
Stars twinkle with frosty light,
Cosmic winds begin to blow,
Whispers of what we can't know.

Galaxies spin with icy grace,
Time stands still in this embrace,
Nebulas glide, softly they sway,
Frosty glimmers mark the way.

Each glimmer tells a tale untold,
Of cosmic wonders, bright and bold,
Through the void, where silence thrums,
The universe speaks, and beauty hums.

Beneath the quilt of the endless sky,
Dreams awaken, as comets fly,
Frosty glimmers, our heartfelt guide,
In cosmic depths, we take our stride.

So gaze upon this starry dome,
Find your place, your cosmic home,
Let the frosty glow ensnare,
In the vastness, find your prayer.

Beneath Ice

Underneath the crystal shell,
Silent secrets, none can tell,
Frozen whispers coat the ground,
In this stillness, peace is found.

Layers thick, with time entwined,
Nature's canvas, purest kind,
Life lies dormant, deeply curled,
Awaiting warmth to fold the world.

Cold embraces every form,
Shielding life from winter's storm,
Beneath ice, the heart still beats,
Waiting for the sun's warm treats.

Icicles hang like frozen dreams,
Catch the light in silver beams,
Beneath the surface, life persists,
In the cold, where hope exists.

When the thaw begins to flow,
Nature wakes, begins to grow,
Underneath, the world will bloom,
Breaking free from winter's gloom.

Stars Remember

In the silence of the night,
Stars gather, holding light,
Echoes of the tales they weave,
Nostalgic dreams, they never leave.

Galaxies waltz in cosmic dance,
Remnants of a timeless chance,
They shimmer with each memory,
A universe in harmony.

Whispers of the ages past,
In their glow, our shadows cast,
Countless stories etched in space,
Stars remember every face.

Lightyears stretch, yet here they stand,
Burning bright, a guiding hand,
In cosmic hearts, we find our way,
Through the night and into day.

So look up at the starry sea,
Feel their warmth, and let it be,
For in their light, we all belong,
Stars remember, forever strong.

A Celestial Chill in Glinting Space

Across the endless, dark expanse,
Stars shimmer in a frozen dance,
A chill embraces cosmic night,
Glinting jewels, purest light.

The universe holds its breath so still,
In icy mists, the void does thrill,
Comets trace their silver paths,
While constellations weave their baths.

Nebulae whisper, soft and low,
Wrapped in dreams from long ago,
A celestial chill we cannot taste,
In the vastness, beauty's laced.

Each twinkle sings a lullaby,
As galaxies kiss the velvet sky,
In glinting space, our spirits rise,
Embraced beneath the cosmic sighs.

So drift among the sparkling night,
Let wonders fill your heart with light,
For in this chill, we find our place,
A home within the endless space.

Whispers of Cosmic Frost

On the twilight of the great expanse,
Whispers of cosmic frost enhance,
A delicate touch on starlit dreams,
Where quiet beauty softly gleams.

Winds of wonder round us swirl,
In this realm, our thoughts unfurl,
Each breath carries tales of old,
As nights unfold their secrets bold.

Icy tendrils wrapped in glow,
Sparkle like the snow below,
Each star a voice that calls to thee,
In the cosmos, we are free.

Frosted light dances and plays,
Illuminating night's embrace,
Guiding hearts that yearn to find,
Connection to the vast, divine.

So listen close, the cosmos speaks,
In frozen words, the heart still seeks,
Whispers of frost, forever true,
In cosmic depths, I search for you.

A Breath of Arctic Light

In the chill of dawn's embrace,
Whispers dance on frozen trails.
Colors bloom in icy space,
Nature weaves its silent tales.

Fragments of the night take flight,
Stars twinkle in the fading frost.
Glowing softly, pure and bright,
Every shadow, now embossed.

Beneath the sky, a world unspun,
Gentle breezes share a sigh.
As this fleeting moment's begun,
Time stands still; the heart can fly.

Glistening like a diamond's sheen,
Waves of light break on the ice.
Frosted land, a canvas clean,
Nature's breath, a sweet device.

In the stillness, secrets hide,
Ancient echoes, soft and clear.
In this beauty, we abide,
Holding memories held dear.

Radiance of Winter's Night

Underneath a blanket bright,
Snowflakes twirl in choir's sway.
Moonlight bathes the world in white,
Night unveils the dreams at play.

Fires crackle, warmth inside,
Stories shared through hazy eyes.
Hearts befall where love will bide,
Magic lingers in the skies.

Stars like gems on velvet beds,
Whispers floating, soft as song.
In the stillness, silence treads,
Winter nights, where we belong.

Breath of coolness touches skin,
Echoing the time so still.
Adventures beckon from within,
In the night, the world we fill.

Radiance, a fleeting glance,
Wonders draped in crystal lace.
In this moment, take the chance,
Feel the magic we embrace.

Glimmering Silence of the Abyss

Deep below the ocean's weave,
Mysteries hide in shadows cold.
Where the light dares not to leave,
Ancient tales of ages old.

Glittering silence swells in blue,
Starlit beings drift and sway.
In the vastness, whispers true,
Secrets thrill in dark ballet.

Flowing currents dance and glide,
Life adorns the silent deep.
In the water, dreams abide,
Hushed reflections softly weep.

Echoes of the moon above,
Journey through the endless night.
Cradled in a world of love,
Hope emerges in the light.

Glimmering pathways stretch away,
In the depths where shadows roam.
In this silence, spirits play,
Finding solace; we are home.

Cosmic Frost on Silent Wings

High above the waking world,
Stars glimmer on a velvet shroud.
In the cosmos gently swirled,
Frosted wings of night are proud.

Celestial whispers through the void,
Night skies echo, soft and clear.
In the grand expanse deployed,
Flames of fate dance ever near.

Galaxies in silence twine,
Crystals shimmering with grace.
In the dark, the light will shine,
Bringing warmth to frozen space.

Time unfolds a cosmic tale,
Endless dreams in starlit streams.
Wonders woven without fail,
Holding tight to midnight dreams.

As the universe takes flight,
Frost on wings begins to sing.
Echoing the depths of night,
In this space, our spirits cling.

An Evening Wrapped in Light

The sun dips low, a golden hue,
Soft whispers dance in twilight's view.
Stars awaken, one by one,
Their twinkling tales have just begun.

A canvas brushed with shades so bright,
As day concedes to gentle night.
Moonlight glimmers on the sea,
A lullaby of serenity.

Crickets sing their evening song,
Nature's chorus, rich and strong.
In this moment, time stands still,
Hearts are hushed, a tranquil thrill.

The breeze, a soft and tender sigh,
Beneath the vast, embracing sky.
Each shadow weaves a tale of grace,
Wrapped in light, a warm embrace.

An evening's gift, so pure and bright,
Enfolds the world in sweet delight.
Lost in wonder, we take flight,
In dreams that bloom in soft twilight.

Frozen Flare of the Heavens

In the stillness of the night,
Stars ignite with flickering light.
Fragments of the cosmos drift,
A shimmering, glistening gift.

A frozen flare in endless space,
Whispers of an ancient grace.
Galaxies swirl, a cosmic dance,
In the blackness, we find our chance.

Nebulas bloom in colors bold,
Stories of the universe told.
Light-years echo in silent song,
Wonders where we all belong.

Time dissolves under celestial gaze,
In the vastness, we stand amazed.
Infinite paths stretch far and wide,
A journey taken with stars as guide.

We feel the pull of the night skies,
Drawing dreams with tender sighs.
In frozen flares, our spirits soar,
Chasing wonders forevermore.

Wisp of the Cosmic Breath

A wisp of breath, a cosmic flow,
Through starlit realms, it dances slow.
In the silence, secrets churn,
Whispers of the night we yearn.

Galactic winds caress the void,
Filling hearts once felt destroyed.
A tapestry of dreamers spun,
Each thread a tale, a life begun.

Moonbeams carve a path so bright,
Inviting souls to take their flight.
Past the confines of earthly bounds,
In every heartbeat, freedom sounds.

A shimmer in the quiet air,
An echo of a wishful prayer.
With every breath, the cosmos sighs,
In the dance of stars, the heart replies.

Together we weave our dreams anew,
On the canvas where wishes grew.
In the expanse of endless night,
A wisp of breath ignites our light.

Frostbitten Fables of the Skies

Beneath the frost-kissed, pale blue,
Whispers of tales long overdue.
Among the clouds, the echoes play,
Fables of night, drifting away.

Each flake that falls, a story told,
In winter's grasp, the dreams unfold.
Mountains wear their icy crowns,
While starlit skies weave jewel gowns.

In the chill, our hearts ignite,
Frostbitten dreams take soaring flight.
The moon, a lantern, guides our quest,
As we find warmth in the coldest jest.

Scraps of laughter float in the breeze,
Carried on whispers through the trees.
In frostbitten fables, love abounds,
In every glance, eternity grounds.

We trace the patterns in the snow,
With each step, our spirits grow.
Fables of the skies, a tender call,
In winter's embrace, we find it all.

Velvet Nights and Icy Gleams

In velvet nights, the stars align,
Glistening softly, pure and fine.
Whispers echo through the trees,
A gentle touch, the winter breeze.

Moonlit paths where shadows dance,
Embrace the silence of the chance.
Dreams unfold in frosty air,
A moment held, beyond compare.

Crimson hues of dusk will fade,
As twilight comes, the night's parade.
Each breath a ghost, both sweet and raw,
In stillness found, a sacred law.

Gems of frost on windows cling,
While distant bells of winter ring.
Every heartbeat feels alive,
With velvet nights, our spirits thrive.

In icy gleams, our souls ignite,
Embracing darkness, chasing light.
Together we will find our way,
In velvet nights that softly sway.

Stars Adrift in Arctic Seas

Stars adrift in arctic seas,
Shimmer bright through winter's freeze.
Waves of magic, cold and deep,
In silence wrapped, the world will sleep.

Neon flares in midnight's sky,
Touch the hearts of those who sigh.
Guiding ships with ancient lore,
To distant shores, forevermore.

Frosty breath on ocean's tide,
In the darkness, dreams abide.
A tapestry of light is spun,
In the twilight, we are one.

Sparkling trails on frozen seas,
Kissed by breath of northern breeze.
The firmament sings crystal songs,
In icy realms where hope belongs.

Stars alight, a fleeting glance,
Encourage hearts to take a chance.
In arctic air, the night will weave,
A story that we dare believe.

Celestial Breezes Beneath Frozen Skies

Celestial breezes touch the night,
Beneath frozen skies, a wondrous sight.
Echoes of starlight, soft and clear,
Guide the hearts that hold them dear.

Whispers travel on the wind,
Through the dreams that fate has pinned.
Each gentle gust, a kiss of grace,
In frozen realms, we find our place.

Glistening snowflakes start to fall,
Carpeting earth, a jeweled shawl.
In the hush, we make our vow,
To cherish moments, here and now.

Veils of mist begin to rise,
Painting portraits in the skies.
In twilight's glow, we softly breathe,
As celestial tales we weave.

Beneath the frost, our spirits soar,
In unity, we crave for more.
With every sigh of night's embrace,
We dance together, time and space.

Ethereal Chill of Cosmic Wonder

Ethereal chill, a cosmic tune,
In the cradle of the moon.
Glacial whispers fill the void,
Mysteries of space, unalloyed.

In shadows deep, the starlight plays,
Lighting up the darkest ways.
Time stands still, as hearts will race,
In chill's embrace, we find our place.

Galaxies swirl in muted hues,
An endless dance of vibrant blues.
Each moment stretches, soft and wide,
In cosmic wonder, we confide.

Falling stars may drift away,
But their brilliance will always stay.
In every heart, a spark remains,
To guide us through our joys and pains.

Infinity wraps around our souls,
In the beauty that life unfolds.
With ethereal chill, we rise anew,
In cosmic wonder, just me and you.

Milton Keynes UK
Ingram Content Group UK Ltd.
UKHW021045031224
452078UK00010B/592